OTHERWISE

# OTHERWISE, MY LIFE IS ORDINARY

*Bobby Byrd*

P O E M S

Cinco Puntos Press
*El Paso*

Many thanks to the editors and to the supporters of the magazines, newspapers, bus systems and book publishers where versions of several of these poems appeared—*Puerto del Sol* (Rus Bradburd); *Mezcla: Art & Writing from the Tumblewords Project* (Donna Snyder, editor; Mouthfeel Press 2009); *El Paso Times* (Ramón Rentería); El Paso Sun Metro Public Transit, in association with El Paso Public Library (Jack Galindo); *The Big Bridge* Online Magazine (Hal Johnson); *House Organ Poetry Magazine*; and especially Longhouse Publications (Bob and Susan Arnold, editors and proprietors), which has supported and published my poetry for decades.

FIRST EDITION
10 9 8 7 6 5 4 3 2 1

Library of Congress Cataloging-in-Publication Data

Byrd, Bobby, 1942-
  [Poems. Selections]
  Otherwise my life is ordinary : poems / by Bobby Byrd. —
First Edition.
      pages cm
  ISBN 978-1-935955-75-7 (Paperback : alk. paper)
  I. Title.

PS3552.Y66A6 2014
811'.54—dc23

                    2013040641


Book design: JB Bryan / La Alameda Press

# { CONTENTS }

*Always for Lee.*

*And for our children and grandchildren.*

*This book, in its way, is a celebration for them.*

# HOW DID THIS HAPPEN?

*in memory of Paul Blackburn, mentor and friend*

A FEW YEARS AGO, Joy Harjo gave me her business card. Our friendship began back to the 1970s when we were both in Albuquerque. We were both young poets, unsteady in who we were. Our oldest children, both daughters, went to kindergarten together. But now we were in Tucson in the spring at a book festival. Those same daughters are now over 40. The sun was hot, the sky so very desert blue. We talked about old friends and families and poets and poetry. After we said goodbye, I looked at the back side of her card. It said, "The path has its own intelligence." I had a little epiphany right then. *I am a poet.* That's what I do. I laughed out loud. It was strange getting such a message on a business card.

A path, depending on the terrain, goes this way, then it goes that way. To explain it is impossible. To say one thing is to deny another. So what is said is wrong. And then it changes. But, I am a poet, language is my business, and I think that I have a deep-seated, almost organic, poetics that lets me follow the meandering path. This poetics of mine is like a three-legged donkey. A goofy-looking pack animal that stumbles along beside me. Damn thing just materialized haphazardly when I was growing up.

I used to tell my kids, and now I tell my grandkids, that I'd be dead without black music. Race music. 1950s Memphis music. It was a cultural revolution for us white kids growing up in the South. Sure, I drank too much, but I learned not to trust God-speak, I learned not to trust politic-speak, I learned to shake my hips and listen to the music. Listen real closely. That's the only way to learn how to dance. Sex turned out to be okay after all.

If somebody told me different, I didn't trust them. Black people taught me that. I started paying attention to black people. My imagination opened up. My heart opened up. If somebody told me I was going down a dead end, I didn't trust them. Black culture and its music were at the heart of my rite of passage. I climbed up through the smoke hole into the night sky.

Then my friend Harvey Goldner introduced me to the Beats and the New American poetry, all the weird and wonderful use of all kinds of language and words—street words, curse words, found words, conversations, black words, white words, any kind of words—that we can plug into poems and say what the hell we want. Let the words find out what we want to say. This could be the language of my own poetry. Harvey gave me that gift.

And from the beginning, I was buoyed up by woman-consciousness. I didn't plan it that way. It just happened. My father William Byrd (aka "Billy" to my mother and to his friends) was a pilot contracted to the U.S. Army to teach young airmen the skills for flying combat missions in the wars against Germany and Japan. But one day his little two-seater plane, with a student pilot aboard, took a nosedive into the ground. Both men were killed. It was 1945. We were living in Clarksdale, Mississippi. Our world shifted. My brother, two sisters and I were raised by our widowed mother, Charlotte Stanage Byrd, and our African-American maid, Darthula Baldwin. When I was a baby, I couldn't say "Darthula," so I said "Tula." The name stuck. She was Tula for us all. And, I, as the youngest man-child, assumed the position of Tula's favorite.

The two women became, within our household, close friends and confidantes. I fought with them, argued with them, but through it all, they were feeding me woman-heart intravenously. A strange drug. I didn't know what happened to me. They fed my heart and understanding. I could look into different places because I could feel things different. That's where my path began.

*"Earth Angel, Earth Angel, will you be mine?"*

★

This is how I write a poem, but today it's not a poem.
It's like a little story.
That happens sometimes.

Now it's Sunday afternoon. Earlier I was on my hands and knees, clumsy old man with a bum hip, pulling treacherous Bermuda grass out of the garden. The goddamn stuff won't grow where I want it to grow, but it certainly loves to journey into places I don't want it. My old man skin was bleeding here and there from the scratches and pricks. The blood doesn't bother me. In fact, I like seeing my blood, as long as it's in these small doses seeping out of my body. I like sucking it off my skin.

I was in that corner of the yard where the Texas laurel and the Banks Yellow Rose explore their particular niche of urbanized desert geography. Back in March, I had stuffed an aloe plant behind them in the darkest spot, where it could get water and enjoy the shade. I must remember the poor thing when the freezes come.

I want our gardens to seem overcrowded and sloppy, like jungles, but without the Bermuda. Lee is just the opposite. She likes organizing and pruning plants. In Portland once, we went to the beautiful Japanese Zen garden there, and she came out lecturing me about pruning and minimalism. "Yeah, yeah," I said, caught once again in my contradictions. I'm supposed to be the Zen Buddhist, but my gardening aesthetic loves riotous redneck fecundity. Even in the desert.

Forty-five years now, our aesthetics have always clashed like this. She likes everything neat and orderly, her stories with perfect endings; and I enjoy the everyday chaos, my desk a mess, a story line unraveling in an unexpected place and going maybe nowhere. And besides, she is a Christian and I do Zen—Lee praying to God and me staring at a wall. It's our own koan:

*The Christian and the Zen Buddhist are married.*
*Which one is wrong? Which one is right?*
*Old Mumon said, if you answer one way or the other,*
*everything is lost.*

That question burned in my stomach for years. The anger in my heart was like a skin rash. It wouldn't go away. Not anger toward Lee, but toward Christianity. It was part of the baggage of growing up in the South. But over time—finding quiet and staring at the wall, living my life,—I realized that when Lee and I made love, the Buddha and Jesus would go off into the other room and close the door behind them. They'd go for long walks in the neighborhood and chat about the people who lived in all the houses. Sometimes they'd be gone for days. And it wasn't only love-making where they would make themselves scarce. It might happen at dinner time. Lee and I would sit down to a lovely meal. I had cooked some black beans, she had tossed a fresh salad with all sorts of goodies, plus she had baked a skillet full of cornbread juicy with butter. We had chopped tomatoes, onion and cilantro to garnish the beans. Some salsa. We'd share a bottle of wine and chat about our kids and grandkids. We'd hold hands. The evening light would be perfect, the world would be perfect. Jesus and the Buddha would be hiding in the bushes with their mouths shut. They didn't want to bother us.

Old Mumon listened to my stories and he read my poems. He'd ask me questions from time to time. Are you still angry? What's more important? What's the difference between Jesus and the Buddha anyway? Especially after you scrape off all the words and the rest of the hoopla? The old monk would grunt and shake his old shaved head. I'd go sit and stare at a wall. One day he just up and disappeared. I haven't seen old Mumon in a long time now.

★

So that's how I write poetry. I'm doing something, like working in the garden, and the experience somehow opens up my imagination. William Carlos Williams would understand. And like that dead plum-eating poet, I start following the words towards a conclusion that, when I'm done, *feels* like a poem. At least for the time being. Then, over time, I play with the words. This is fun stuff. I say the words out loud. I move them around. Computers are cool for playing with words. I don't worry too much about "meaning." I don't worry too much about losing stuff. The poem, I feel, will take care of itself. A few short sentences may become a four-page poem; a four-page poem may become two or three lines. I've learned to trust myself. I trust my poetics, that old three-legged beast that's been packing my baggage all this time. And I'm always surprised—when the poem gets in a book or I read it aloud in front of real people—that the poem works. That it somehow makes sense.

No matter what, I can only write my own poems. That seems like a silly thing to say, but it took me years to learn this simple lesson. Reading poets all these years, especially my favorites, helped me to learn this lesson. Also, old grumpy Barney Childs, who taught the only two poetry-writing classes I ever took. He used to ask me, "Do you know which direction the wind is blowing today?" He would be pissed if I didn't know. He's the same guy who wadded up the first poem I ever turned into his class. He tossed it in the garbage.

My poetics are simple enough. Nothing new really. No manifesto. I believe in those experiences that open up holes of understanding. Sometimes it's a word or phrase spoken on the street; other times I can be watching a beetle climbing lonesome down a concrete curb or my beloved and I can be making love. I think of these times as a spiritual experience because I let go.

My mechanical and habitual ways of seeing drop away. It's a spark of some kind. Or, like Whitman said, the mind becomes like leaves of grass. The wind blows through those grasses. I start playing with the first few words. I listen carefully to the words. I say them out loud.

I learned a long time ago that the lyrical "I" in my poems is not me. That was a relief. It allowed me to lie. To move away from what may or may not have happened. Who cares if it happened or not? Instead, I go looking for words and events that "make sense." Sometimes the words are the exact opposite of the first words that found their way into my poem-making. Death might become life, black might become light. The same with events. Truth is not what happened. Better to let the poem happen. And I know that whatever happens inside the poem could not have happened without what has gone before in my own life—the poems, the pieces of my life, the poems and poetics of those poets who have been so important to me, the books I have read, the hours and hours I have sat zazen, and always the understanding that my body gives me.

Yes, yes, I know I'm contradicting myself.

And I've learned after all this time that writing poetry is a wonderful occupation. It pays next to nothing, but that's okay and was to be expected. Still, because I write poetry, I met and married Lee, we have wonderful children and grandchildren, Lee and I became independent book publishers, I became a practitioner and later a teacher of Zen Buddhism, and I have wonderful, interesting and close friends. Many of these friendships stretch back for decades. There have been grief and troubles along the way for all of us. Terrible struggles. Terrible grief. But also incredible joy and flashes of understanding. At the heart of it all is an ordinary life. I am a husband, father and grandfather. A regular householder. Being 70-plus now, I can look back on it and it feels like a very natural path to get here where I am typing this. The mockingbirds are chattering outside. The November day is cold and bright. Joy's message was right. This path, like any river, has its own intelligence. I'm still walking beside the stumbling donkey. A weird three-legged creature, but I love her. She tells me who I am. She leads me downhill. I'm writing poems. It's what I do.

# KOAN

The Roshi makes shitty coffee.

## SACRED RITUAL

Blood in your stools?

No.

How many times do you get up to pee at night?

2 times usually. Sometimes 3. Sometimes none.

How is your sex life?

Not as good as it used to be.

# A SHORT HISTORY OF OUR MARRIAGE
## FOR OUR GRANDCHILDREN

Forgive us. We didn't have a plan.
We had instead a blue Ford window van,
1960, six-cylinder. Sometimes we took out the backseat
And put in a mattress or a raggedy couch.
Once we put in everything we owned,
Even that black R-60 BMW motorcycle—

We headed off to God-knows-where.
Colorado, it turned out, and three kids
Who became your mother or fathers,
Your aunt, your uncles. Somewhere we
Have an old suitcase where we put
All of our secrets. But don't go looking for it.

The suitcase doesn't exist. It's only words.
Like these words are my words.
Your grandmother has her own words.
Her words tell the same story, but her story
Is different. That's the way we all are.
I hope someday you understand.

# WE HAD A FEW THINGS TO SAY

RELIEVE ME

OF THE BONDAGE

OF MY SELF

That's what her tatt announced centered in that lovely soft space
Between her shoulder blades, slit by her spine. Sans Serif
Ariel Black & Bold. Ink Lady. Purple lips. Purple nails.
A grey tank top that advertised absolutely
Nothing except
Her breasts. She was waiting for
Her soy cappuccino with an extra shot at the Epic Café,
4th and University in Tucson, Arizona.
I was waiting for my Americano.

"Lots of room?"

"Lots and lots of room."

Oh, she was so young. My duty was to be the wise old man.
I told her to stay away from Gutei.
"That crazy old monk will cut off your finger."
She looked at my hands.
She told me that in Tucson the mockingbirds
Are discussing spring again. I said that poetry
Quit being a contact sport when I turned 60.
She said, "the tsunami in Japan."

We wept together. I explained that I sit for real on a zafu
And stare at a wall. Time passes away. It took me years
Just to travel this far. She told me she was a Suicide Girl.

I said, "I love my wife. Our kids are older than you are."
"Nice," she said and smiled those juicy purple lips.

I said, "sweet honey in the rock."
She said, "the balm of Gilead."

She grabbed her soy cap with the extra shot.
Next up was my Americano. Lots and lots of room.

"Perfect," I said. She said, "Goodbye."

# BENNY HAS GONE TO LIVE WITH THE ANGELS

Our neighbor Cecilia Ledesma told my wife
That in the middle of the night her dead husband
Benny still pulls at her sheets. "He's lonely,"

She says, "*mi probrecito*, he's cold. He wants me
To keep him warm." And he follows her to the Senior Center
Like yesterday.

Ceci saw Benny's shadow haunting the dirty yellow walls.
She was dancing sexy la cumbia with that Señor Apodaca.

*Alle tinbalero baila conmigo este song*
*alle tinbailero este la cumbia del sol*

Benny was a wonderfully handsome man. Muy guapo.
But he was a jealous man. He had a desperate shyness.
The shyness made him a drunk. An ugly bad drunk.

He didn't like America. It stole away his power.
Ceci wore tears like jewelry dripping from her obsidian eyes.
"Benny should go away in peace. *Hace dos años ya.*

"He wants me to cross over there with the angels.
I don't want to go. Not yet." Ceci doesn't want to be cold
Like Benny is cold. That's the story Lee told me.

That's a weird story, I told Lee, and forgot about it.
Then the other night I heard Benny on his front porch
Arguing with his old friend, you know, that old vato

Tall and distinguished, like a Mexican-style
Marlboro Man, long silver-black hair combed back
Into a Brylcreem ducktail. But he had no teeth.

And no pickup anymore. Death took his pickup away.
So him and Benny were drinking beer and arguing
Like they used to do. Benny had a plan:

They were going to steal the car keys from Ceci.
He wanted him and his friend to drive away into the nowhere.
The booze was their courage, like old times. It was now

or never. Benny had already learned that there are
no angels, only the stars way up there in the emptiness.
He's too afraid to walk through that door.

And then where would he be?

*Alle tinbalero baila conmigo este song*
*Alle tinbailero este la cumbia del sol*

# THE GREAT CONGRESSIONAL BUDGET BATTLE OF APRIL 2011

The Democrats and Republicans were yelling at each other.
While they bickered, I was digging a hole in the backyard and
I hit a thick layer of caliche one foot down.
Caliche is like concrete, is like greed, is like a curse
Against deep-rooted plants. I don't want the poor to be poorer
And digging in the earth is personal business so
I got a wrecking bar and a shovel. I got dirty and
Sore. I'm an old man. Three weeks it took, a little bit
Every day, a few whacks with the wrecking bar,
Some shovelfuls of caliche.

My son Johnny helped me and Gabriel helped me.
Not the angel Gabriel but the guy who works for me.
This Gabriel doesn't bring any messages from God,
But that's okay, he's a nice guy and he brings me
Sad stories from the Drug Wars in Juárez instead—
The thugs killed the ice cream man,
"They" killed a cop,
"They" killed a man and a woman on Avenida Juárez.
Stories so sad nobody should have to tell them,
Nobody should have to hear them, nobody
Should have to witness them. Embody them.
Especially the children. Children
Like Gabriel's two sons Bryan and Zen.

I planted an olive tree for peace in our world,
Especially in Juárez.
I planted a red flowering plum tree for beauty in our world,
Especially in Juárez.
I want to walk in Peace and Beauty.
I pray that my labors will bear fruit,
But, if not, then I'll plant something different next year.
Yes, I want to be here next year,
Digging holes, planting trees, making prayers.

# KENSHŌ DOWN ON TEXAS AVENUE, EL PASO, TEXAS

When I was a 17-year-old kid in Memphis
I was a Kerouac, Ginsberg and Gary Snyder junkie
So it was natural I got hooked on Zen too.
But I was in Memphis where nothing seemed to happen
So I was sure Zen and *kenshō* grew best in San Francisco
Or maybe the Colorado mountains, maybe even New York City,
Places like that where the enlightened Zen roshis
Liked to go hang out with all the cool people.
That was fifty years ago and today
I ate at the Mexican Cottage on Texas Avenue,
El Paso, Texas of all places
Where they ran a Thursday lunch special on *kenshō*.
I had walked the several blocks from work.
Monsoon clouds in the east.
Even in the downtown the desert smelled like rain,
I gave an old man a couple of dollars to buy himself a burrito.
A cop sat at the counter drinking a beer.
He had served his city.
He was done for the day.
The bitchy waitress Norma
Put the *kensho* in front of me with a smile.
Buen provecho, she said,
Completely out of touch with who she usually is.
She served it up with hot corn tortillas,
Refried beans and a glass of water.

I stared at the food.

May I be worthy of this meal, I whispered.

The afternoon light was coming through the window.

The universe did a little waltz.

ONE two three. ONE two three.

I let go.

Yes, it was me who sat there and breathed and ate.

Don't get me wrong.

The food was good but nothing special.

I had to get back to work.

Our business, like always, is in danger of going belly up.

# THE GUY SAID I LET MY POEMS GO ON TOO LONG

I told him I shouldn't have read Jimmy Schuyler
I shouldn't have read Frank O'Hara
I shouldn't have read Eileen Myles
Even Walt Whitman that old fart
He smelled like dirt
Why is Philip Whalen staring at the white stucco wall?

And they're all queer
Their sexual memory twisting the syntax
Down into the rabbit hole under the tree

*Alice where are you I loved you*
*Bite me eat me love me*

Otherwise my life is ordinary
House sparrows and house finches
Once I was looking out the bedroom window
A Baltimore oriole bright
Like a black and yellow flag among the leaves
Then that one morning a smallish hawk
I think it was a Cooper's I don't know for sure
I was so excited my heart pumping
The backyard was quiet all the little birds
Had disappeared the silence of their chatter
The window into our bedroom
Lee and I have made sacred with our love-making

Disappointments and sorrow
Like clouds passing through the desert sky
And so we have grown old
The proof of the pudding
The light changes
Morning light Electric light Candle light
Jimmy Schuyler would understand
He sits on a sofa on the cover of a book
Frank is lost forever on Fire Island
Eileen is walking Rosie her dog in her poem head
Philip dead asleep on his zafu
Heroic Walt is sniffing at his underarms
Always the sky and the earth
So what if a poem goes on too long?
It's not my fault.

# HARVEY FLOATS THROUGH THE GATE

The fucking butcher in the hospital cut out
Harvey's cancerous tongue.
Harvey hated hospitals. Public sorrow and anger
Were refuges for Harvey, and without his tongue
His bitching was insufficient.
He was breathing and eating out of tubes.
The whole exercise was boring and depressing.
Machines beeped and blinked.
They talked to Harvey like preachers,
They explained the logos of digitized apocalypse.
Take television, for instance.
"Fuck no."
Harvey didn't want to watch television.
His daughters visited with their blue eyes and sad teary faces.
They were so beautiful.
His poet friends couldn't make a decent joke even
In the Face of Death.
"Hello, Death."
He cried. They cried. Life was going nowhere.
Then Harvey's body, without its Captain, decided to let go.
The damn thing began to jump off the diving board.
Harvey grabbed hold.
He didn't want to be left behind.
But he felt like, well, like he was populating
One of his silly poems.
He kicked some, he groaned,

But after a while, he began to enjoy the ride.

"Cool," he thought, "maybe I have been right about some things."

He was glad he was sober.

The view was so much better.

## BACK ROADS TO FAR TOWNS

I wish old Bashō would come to my house.
Especially when it's winter, a paltry desert winter,
Warm enough this evening to sit outside in the city night
Huddled up in a warm jacket and a good hat
The trees bare-boned,
Old men, Bashō and me—
We will drink some red wine
A bottle of the $7.49 merlot from the 7/11
The one with the yellow kangaroo
And we'll swap stories.
Like that one about the frog jumping into the pond.
Splash!
What's the story behind that, huh?
Or maybe he'll want to know,
What's it like to be pissing in the backyard with my two sons
The full moon like a Chinese coin.
Ha!
We'll sit there on our sorry asses
Open-mouthed
At the beauty of a dying cockroach
We'll write a few poems
Three-liner thingamabobs
Old-man fingers
Useless 3x5 index cards
I'll lose somewhere
Why not?

The gate swings open and shut
Open and shut
The cockroach is the gatekeeper
Bashō and me
We will empty that bottle of wine

*"Enough," he says, "is always exactly enough."*

"That's a good one," I say, and we giggle
And the big bright moon
Dodges back and forth behind the clouds.

## LA LUZ DE LA RESISTENCIA—
## A LIGHT POEM IN MEMORY OF RAUL SALINAS

Raul,

Tonight there's a little bit of moonlight in El Paso.
A cup of light.
The city lights have dimmed the starlight.
My city wastes away.

That's what you did, brother.
Disappeared into the Milky Way forever light.
That's what happens, no?
You have left us with a little bit of your death light.

The sad light of poverty.
The angry light of poverty.
Do some drugs kind of light.
Sell some drugs kind of light.
You studied yourself in prison light.
You studied the machine in that same prison light.
The beast of civilization light.
15 years of incandescent light.
Florescent light.
Naked light.
You learned you had enough light to read a book.
Enough light to make a newspaper.
Enough light to write a poem.

You were such a little man to have so much light.
Chicano-jazz vato hipster light.
Enough light to make the world new.
Enough light to give you the chance to grow old.

You said:

> *I go to talk to those kids.*
> *They listen to me.*
> *Those kids listen to me.*
> *I will be their friend.*
> *I will be your friend.*

What kind of light is manifesto light?
What kind of light is peace light?
What kind of light is resistance light?
What kind of light is compassion light?
What kind of light is man light?
What kind of light is woman light?
What kind of light is poem light?

# FOR LOVE ON I-10, WEST TEXAS

Ivan Ilych was dead before we got to Ozona.

He had answered his koan.

His bones began to rattle like my mother's had rattled

(her frail hand in mine, her blue eyes)

And then, like my mother, Ivan Illych let go.

Same thing with Robert Creeley.

He died up north of here in Odessa—

Strange place for a Yankee poet to die.

Especially Creeley,

No big car to drive, his hip New England riff

Useless in all this emptiness of sky.

Then our van ran out of gas.

A sheriff's deputy—

Big square-jawed man in a cowboy hat—

Showed up with 5 gallons in a red plastic can.

He had two sidekicks, a Chicano and a black guy.

Texas is always surprising me.

All three of them nursing an adrenalin rush.

Big smiles all around.

They wanted to help somebody.

Anybody.

They had just cleaned up a bloody mess on the highway.

An SUV going east, a young couple and their three kids,

The front right tire blew out, the vehicle rolled

Over.

And over.

It was ugly, the black deputy said.

And bloody.

The darkness surrounds us. What

Can we do against it?

Nothing.

Nothing at all.

I thanked them for the gas.

We shook hands all around.

I didn't ask how many people were killed.

I didn't want to know.

What kind of news would that be?

How would it get us to Ozona?

Nothing to do but drive, he said,

And for Christ's sake,

Look out where you're going.

# GROWING UP IN MEMPHIS, #3

In 1952 Dewey Phillips invented Elvis.
It happened on the radio.
Rock n' Roll saved my life.
In 1960 the bad guys sold Elvis into slavery.
Don't let anybody tell you different.

# IN SEARCH OF GOD AT THE THUNDERBIRD BAR
## —PLACITAS, NM 1970

Steve was sitting on a bench nursing a beer when a cowboy walked by. The guy said, "Here, chew on this. You'll go to heaven." Steve crammed three peyote buttons into his mouth. He sat down on a bench and chewed at the stringy foul-tasting cactus. Uggh. They made him want to vomit. The cigarette smoke didn't help. The rock n' roll didn't help. Especially the fucking drums. Things got weirder. Larry the Skinny Poet took off his shirt and started swirling a bullroarer around his head.

Whoosh.

Whoosh.

Whoosh.

Gus the Intellectual of Oz was waving his arms and promising a young lady that he was one of *the best minds of his generation starving hysterical mad...*

A woman sat down next to our hero Steve. She was wearing a hippy dress. No bra. Her breasts flopped around unattended.

"Are you alright, honey?"

He said, "Some cowboy guy gave me three peyote buttons. I think I'm sick."

"Come with me," and she took him by the hand. Outside the air was delicious and cleansing. The moon was in full flower. "It's the Apache Moon," she said. "The harvest is over. It's magic time. Moon time. The Apaches have come down out of the mountains. They want to steal the crops. They want to steal the women."

"Yeah? I don't like that kind of bullshit. The moon is the moon."

"Maybe."

She had a beat-up VW bug, and in the backseat she had a bedroll—a ragged one-person cotton futon and some blankets. She led him out into the chaparral. She laid everything out in the sand and dirt in between a couple of big sage bushes. She pulled off her hippie dress. She was beautiful naked. She and the buffalo grass and the sage bushes. Everything shimmered alive. She said, "Come here." He stumbled in the dirt, pulling off his clothes. He lay down on top of her and they made love together under moon and the stars. The desert shines holy in the moonlight. Maybe she was right about the moon. His body and mind fell away. Maybe she was a goddess. Maybe she had stolen his soul. Then he crawled to the edge of the blankets and puked. Puked out his soul. It slithered away. He wanted the gods to visit him and tell him the truth but they refused. They had better things to do.

"Besides," one said, "there is no truth, not like you want truth."

The woman got up and slipped her dress on. She told him to get up but he couldn't stand. He rolled over and kneeled naked in the moony dirt. She tossed him his clothes, folded up her nest and left him there alone. She didn't even say goodbye.

Steve didn't know what to think
At least it would be a story to tell
He wished his story would end
The earth trembled like jelly

He wondered where his soul had gone to
The bugs clattered in the night
He didn't like heaven
He was worried about snakes
He lost all his love for the moonlight
He wished the sky would rain.

# THIS IS NOT A HAIKU

I've had enough wine for one man.
The Queen of America is waiting for me.
And I saw your penis.
It was right there.

# ELEGY ON THE DEATH OF MY BIG BROTHER

*The preacher said, "Let us pray."*

The preacher sermonized on my brother's drunkenness. The preacher said that my brother Bill had let alcoholism become the meaning of his life. This is why my brother hated religion.

The preacher didn't know—wouldn't understand—that my brother had learned to love God. Even when he was sitting in the woods sucking at his vodka and orange juice. That's why he had told the preachers with all their words and their prayers to leave him alone. He would talk with God instead.

God lived alone in the dark woods of Mississippi. Especially in the winter time when the earth was damp and cold.

Many hours my brother sat in those woods, his rifle or shotgun cupped in his hands like a lover. He waited for the deer, the rabbits, the squirrels and the birds. He had learned since childhood to feed on their flesh but as he grew into an old man, he understood that he loved the wild animals. He was killing what he loved.

This was the koan of his life.

Animal blood seeped warm from his hands into the earth. For years, my brother, who sat alone in the silence of the woods, had begun talking to himself. At first, he thought he was whispering to his gun, but no, he was whispering to a lost place inside himself. A wild place that needed no words. And while he waited, he found wild mushrooms and learned their names. He bought books and studied photographs. He ate the mushrooms, careful not to poison himself or his sons and his grandchildren who loved to eat at his table. He cooked the mushrooms with venison and rabbit and fish and squirrel. Onions and lots of garlic and tomatoes and all sorts of spices. Gravy and biscuits and black-eyed peas.

Oh, he was a good cook. An old-fashioned white man backwoods Southern cook. My children, when they were little, loved Uncle Bill's hush puppies fried deep in lard. And they loved my brother. They didn't know about his sorrow and his alcoholism. To them he was a mysterious man who loved to be alive with food and laughter.

*Uncle Bill, Uncle Bill, tell us a story.*

Sure enough, God heard my brother whispering. God listened deeply. God wants us all to sit in the dark woods all alone. So God began talking to my brother. They met in a secret place where there was a dead stump for my brother to sit on. The ground was thick with dead leaves rotting into the earth. Mushrooms poking up like sperm out of the mud and dank leaves. Sacred ground. God taught my brother many things. Especially about the woods. How each moment to the next is totally new and fresh. Totally independent. Totally perfect. Each moment exists only in his own mind. No one else's. And without reason.

Yes, that's true, my brother said. And he shut his eyes and prayed.

But my brother couldn't stop drinking the vodka and orange juice. He brought along a little silver flask every time he met with God. He blamed his drunkenness on God. Surely, God could do something. But God would do nothing. It was not his job.

And after a long while, God ran out of patience with my brother. That was okay. My brother was angry with God too. He didn't trust God anymore. God had taken away his sex. He couldn't make love anymore. Couldn't get it up. God and my brother said goodbye.

Years passed like that. My brother had become lonely again in the woods without God. The dead stump in the dark woods was no longer a holy place. It was quiet and peaceful but something had seeped away.

*What was death anyway?*

The wild animals had taught him about death. My brother had seen so many animals die. They had been his guide into where the darkness begins. But they left something out. The gate didn't swing open.

Then, suddenly, God showed up again.

My brother and God spent hours together. They murmured strange guttural sounds at each other. They were like the animals, on their hands and knees, sniffing at the air and the earth.

Be patient, God said.

Walk in beauty, God said.

Walk in peace, God said.

Walk in beauty, God said.

The next morning my brother was anchored in his flat-bottomed boat in a backwater on the Mississippi River. It was his favorite spot, tucked into some bushes twenty feet from the bank just down river from a bend. The water was still, but a stone's throw from where he sat the big river churned and roiled. He had been there since an hour before dawn. He had his shotgun cupped in his hands. He was sipping at his vodka and orange juice. He heard them coming. A line of mallards flew over his left shoulder. He aimed, he led the ducks like our Papaw had taught him when he was a little boy. He squeezed the trigger. Blam. He pumped the empty shell hissing into the water. Blam. Again. Blam. My brother shot three out of the sky. He gathered them up and waited again. And again the ducks came. Blam. Blam. That was the limit. That was the law. My brother began to cry as these last two ducks fell and splashed into the still water.

Maybe my brother knew that his time too had come to its end. Maybe God had told him. Maybe he knew all by himself. Or maybe he understood that God and that wild place inside were one and the same. That place that needed no words. The place of silence.

Maybe he knew nothing of what awaited him.

He was done. He dragged his boat onto its trailer. He tossed the wet ducks, their beautiful long necks hanging loose like cut pieces of rope, into the back of his truck. He climbed into the cab and turned on the ignition.

My brother's heart exploded inside the shell of his body.

That was supposed to be the end. That was the end.

This is how my brother learned to love God.

*Now I can say goodbye to my brother Bill.*

# IN MEMORY OF A FAMOUS POET, 2010

"Being a famous poet
Is not like being famous."
—*John Ashbery*

If I moved three miles south into Mexico

(I live in El Paso)

I could be shot for being a poet.

In fact, I could be shot for being alive.

Dead, I would be innocent.

That's what Amado Carrillo Fuentes said.

"Only the dead are innocent."

He died on an operating table trying to get a new face.

He no longer wanted to be himself.

But Amado was not a poet.

He was a narco-traficante and a murderer.

A vicious and evil man.

Although now he is innocent according to his own definition.

Me, I could be dead for the sin of being a poet.

For the sin of being alive.

Guilty, as charged.

Maybe I would also be famous then.

At least for a couple of days.

My wife would be weeping on CNN.

She'd sell a few of my poetry books.

## POEM TO AN ESTRANGED FRIEND
## AUGUST 2007

Lee reads the newspaper obituaries when she has the chance.
The deaths of random people scattered like fables
                                        here and there
            throughout the city.

                    So the other day

she read that *you* are dead...

                    She said your name,

            she paused,

                            she said,

            "Not *our...*"

                        and she said your name again

            making sure I knew

                        it was a man who shared your name.

Yet, in that brief instant
I grieved for you.

Your resurrection, although ordinary and funny even,
was a delightful happiness.
We laughed together, she and I,
relieved that you are alive and well although
we have not seen you and talked with you in such a long time.

Such is human anger.
I cannot even remember what my anger is about.
I could if I tried but I don't want to try.
Do you remember?
Words were said.

Then I went about my day and forgot about you
like I am sure you have forgotten about me.

             You and me.
             Me and you.

I have a friend, a man a few years older than me.
"Henry" his name is and he lives in Houston.
I really don't have any friends named "Henry" but
"Henry" is a real friend and the name
is good enough for this occasion. Henry's heart
is leaking blood inside the tabernacle of his body.
"Congenital heart disease."
Henry smiles.
Knowledge, he says, helps. And yes, he's afraid sometimes
especially going to bed alone

looking up at the ceiling fan whirring round.
"Every night my life is diminished by one day."
Henry vows not to squander the next day.
He takes his medications and lives his life.
He is waiting.

One night he told me a secret.
We had been sipping at a good but inexpensive Spanish red wine.
Not much. Just enough. Like old men do.
We had gone outside his house
to piss into the jungle of his garden.

A hot and humid evening, you know how
the heat in East Texas is so horrible in August.
We saw the North Star through the trees
and the haze of the city lights. Henry, like Lee, enjoys
reading the obits when he has the chance.
Usually on the toilet first thing in the morning.
Then one day he read where
he himself had died of a heart attack.
The same name, the same middle initial,
even born the same year,
the same month, but two weeks earlier.

Henry laughed.

The obituary was about a black man.

He could tell from the dead man's long list of accomplishments.

That's when he told me his secret, a gift from his father—

"I am a racist," he said.

He carries a furtive loathing for black people,

is desperately afraid of black men,

like when he sees them at the Stop 'N Go,

standing in line to buy a quart of beer.

He has tried many things to cure himself,

but the secret remains there, like DNA,

a stain on his leaking heart.

Henry keeps his secret close and hidden.

He is a public man in a small way.


The dead man had done good in his life.

He owned an insurance company, he was a deacon in his church,

and he had many friends who loved him.

Henry went to the funeral.

The casket was open, the services had not begun,

The dead man smelled like flowers and sandalwood.

Henry knelt at the casket

and prayed for the soul of the man who shared his name.

He prayed for his own soul.

He wept.

The chapel was full and a woman began to play the organ.

My friend stood and shook hands with the widow, bent

and kissed her on the cheek.

Children and grandchildren nodded to him gratefully,

this white man with tears in his eyes.

That's the end of Henry's story

      and he laughed
              like it was a joke
         a mistake

but we both knew it wasn't a joke, it wasn't a mistake.
He wants to learn to forgive and love himself before he dies.
That's what he told me.

A train's horn was screaming, going west or east,
no place in particular. Above us, thousands
of moths and beetles circled the glow of streetlight,
and in that swirling radiance
bats and nighthawks feasted on the insects
—hungry angels ecstatic and awhirl in the holy sacrament of life.
I truly feared and loved what I saw in that night sky.
So terrible, so beautiful.
We went back inside the shelter of Henry's house.
He poured us each a small glass of wine.
"A serviceable wine," Henry said, "but it does the job."

# THIS IS HOW WE BECAME DRUNKS
## MEMPHIS: THE 1950S

*"Nothing ever worked exactly right."*
—Harvey Goldner


Douglas smoked Kools.

Harvey smoked Chesterfields and Luckies.

I smoked Camels and Luckies.

Jimmy smoked Luckies and Pall Malls.


Douglas' father was dead.

My father was dead.

Harvey's father was a wimpy drunk.

Jimmy's father was a mean drunk.


Douglas liked to masturbate into his sock.

Jimmy never confessed.

Harvey said he'd do it anywhere anyhow.

I liked lying in bed with a warm damp washrag.


My mother sold real estate.

Douglas' mother was a secretary.

Harvey's mother was a housewife.

Jimmy's mother worked in a bank.


Douglas worked in a pet store after school.

Harvey wrote poems about death.

I liked sleeping with a gun.
Jimmy hated his father.


Mother sent me to private school.
Douglas shot himself in the leg playing quick draw.
Jimmy joined the army.
Harvey was reading Burroughs and Rechy.


Jimmy came home in a box.
Harvey was a pallbearer.
I was a pallbearer.
Douglas was a pallbearer.


The Army said it was an accident.
We said he killed himself.
His mother said the same thing.
The end.

# JUST CHECKING: A MESSAGE FROM MY COMPUTER

Please be patient.

We are checking your computer for malicious software.

Checking your tax returns.

Checking your temperature.

Checking your heart for greed, hatred and delusion.

Checking your chest of drawers for pornography, prophylactics
and sex toys.

Checking your house for termites, cockroaches, mice
and marijuana.

Checking your children for laziness and oedipal complexes.

Checking your mind for sentimentality, superstitious beliefs
and irrationality.

Checking your blood for HIV, steroid usage and prostate cancer.

Checking your blood pressure for looming death.

Checking your prostate for fun.

Checking your books for bad poetry.

Checking your email for subversive activities.

Checking out your wife for kicks.

Checking your religious beliefs.

Checking your internet usage for illicit sexual activities.

Checking the size of your head.

Checking your shoes and your luggage for explosives.

Checking your hips for arthritis.

Checking your underarms for body odor.

Checking your teeth for tooth decay.

Checking your grandchildren for lice.

Checking your penis for size, disease and semen count.

Checking your medicine cabinet for illegal drugs.

Checking your being for traces of enlightenment.

Checking the prescribed drugs you take every day of your life.

Checking your garden for inch worms, aphids and lady bugs.

Checking your home and office energy usage for sins against

the planet.

Checking your oil.

Checking the air pressure in your tires.

Checking your work for errors, egregious or otherwise.

Checking your stories for the truth.

Checking your purchases at amazon.com and your

borrowing habits from the downtown library

for potential treasonous thoughts and activities.

Checking your soul for soul.

Checking your zazen for the presence of Buddha.

Checking your enemies for weapons.

Checking your friends for weapons.

Checking your registration and inspection stickers.

Checking your patriotism.

Checking your DNA to certify innocence or guilt.

Checking your mortgage and your house insurance.

Checking your citizenship and birth certificate.

Checking your voting record.

Checking your phone conversations for any hint of treason.

Checking to see if this qualifies as a poem.

Checking your family tree for racial purity.

Checking for slippage in your intelligence quotient.

Checking your need to write poetry.

Checking your resume and your alleged academic achievements.

Checking your financial health.

Checking the legality of your Last Will and Testament.

Thank you for your patience.

Have a good day.

## PORTRAIT OF A WOMAN

She is simmering the oatmeal for breakfast
The early morning light
The wooden spoon in her hand
Her hips rocking back and forth—
The pink pajama bottoms, a white pullover
40 years we have found these ordinary rituals
A matrimonial dance
And at night, she is the warm body next to mine
We are happy to be animals together
That too is beautiful
Afloat on this side of nothing
Emptiness
Whatever you want to call it
She snores some and some nights she grunts in her sleep

# POETRY IS WAITING FOR ME IN THE OTHER ROOM

I'm an old man and so it's my job to talk about wooden matches.
It's hard finding them anymore, those Diamond matches,
250 "Strike Anywhere" matches in a nice red, white & blue box.
Stores sell those long plastic lighters.
I use matches to light candles, one
every morning when I meditate. Sometimes in the evenings.
Always when we make love. How many more times
will we make love? I think
about this question when I put the flame
to the wick of the candle.
It flickers and gives dreamy light to the bedroom.
She is standing there. I light
two more candles. I forget
about my questions. She has juicy lips.
My mind falls away. After all this time
our bodies fit so perfectly together.
The candle-lit shadows play along with us.
That was last night. Tonight she will be asleep and at peace
when I finally come to bed. The box says Diamond Matches
are made from the "finest" aspen wood, trees that are
so beautiful, the quaking leaves turning gold
up above our little house in Colorado?
That was 40-something years ago.
Our baby daughter was learning how to walk.
We didn't know what we would do
in our lives. I gathered dry aspen wood

to split for kindling for the cooking fire
and to keep us warm in the cold mornings.
It burned so quick and clean.
I'm glad
Aspen wood makes wonderful matches.
Diamond matches
For the Diamond Match Company
Where business is not what it used to be.

# THE MOCKINGBIRD

It's the middle of the night.
She chatters and screams.
It's spring and all—
Like that's some kind of excuse.

# CHANNELING GARCIA LORCA IN VAN HORN, TEXAS

*"All that has dark sound has duende,*
*that mysterious power that everyone feels*
*but no philosopher can explain."*
—Federico Garcia Lorca

One reason to go to Van Horn is to make poems.
You can't miss.
The town is trying to decide if it's living or dying.
Remember the Comanches? Remember the buffalo?
And now the Mexicans are coming.
The wind doesn't care. It has no memory.
The wind and the wide spaces
The skinny ragged traces of mountains.
And the trucks going east and west on I-10
Like there's always someplace else to be
Someplace that is real like TV is real
Like Phoenix is real
Or Dallas or even the American Dream is real like
The fat woman at the Holiday Inn.
She didn't have any rooms
And we were not Joseph and Mary, for Christ's sake,
Too old for that sort of stuff,
Credit cards in our pockets,
Good grownup grey-haired white people,
So she said that the Best Western was a good bet.
Yes, the man said, we have a room.
The lobby smelled like Bangladeshi curry.
His wife had a glorious red dot in the middle of her forehead.

He gave me a key.

Number 207.

Styrofoam cups and thin white towels.

A soft and springy mattress.

Well, the shower was good, and the water was hot.

Lucky for us.

We had the Clos du Bois cabernet.

Albertson's had it on sale for $13.99.

A special treat.

Sure, we made love.

Why not?

Old people can make love too.

There are tricks.

And there is love.

Our names got lost in the sheets.

Like loose change.

The little death.

A freight train thundered by across the street.

The noise of the air conditioner in the window

Was not quite white enough. But we

Found a deep sleep full with our separate dreams.


*I was in my office at work*

*And it was overflowing with chattering people.*

*Angry people. Confused people.*

*A curly-haired little boy was holding onto my leg.*

*He was not afraid, he was humming a tune.*

*That little boy was me.*

The morning sky was a beautiful desert blue.

A cool breeze, another train.

We got in the car and drove to Austin.

Austin is a shitty place to make poems.

Too many young people, too much money,

They think *duende* is some kind of Spanish ice cream.

# TALKING TO MY WIFE WHO IS AWAY AT CHURCH

Remember that pear tree in Santa Rosa?
That was a long time ago, huh?
Thirty years and something.
It was an August like this is August.
Susie was 3 or 4.
The fields were so hot and dusty,
the Pecos River was a sad little stream that summer,
but in the shade of that big pear tree
the flies and the bugs,
like you and me,
were busy feeding on the juicy pears.
Gurdjieff had sent us and our friends to that place.
Him and that weird Russian guy, Ouspensky.
I won't tell that story.
It's too long.
Just let me say
we were out there in the heat and dust
in search of the miraculous.
It was right there in front of us all the time.
Those pears, the bugs and the heat, our friends,
Our daughter Susie, her brothers to come,
You and me.
I wish you were home this morning.
Already it's so hot.
I promise not to argue about God anymore.
I just want to remind you about those flies and bugs.

The Pecos River and where it came from
and where it was going.
I want to talk about those delicious pears.

# A CAMPBELL'S TOMATO SOUP AUTOBIOGRAPHY

Growing up in the 50s
My mother and Tula fed us
Campbell's Tomato Soup
Because it was cheap and easy.
Soon I was getting drunk and listening to
James Brown and Little Richard.

Then in the 60s and 70s
Campbell's Tomato Soup was
Andy Warhol and Richard Nixon
And the Vietnam War on TV.
I dodged the draft
And wrote poems about death.

The 80s and 90s
Came along and our kids
Susie, Johnny and Andy
Didn't like
Campbell's Tomato Soup very much.
How does a poet make a living?

Then 9/11. All those
Dead people falling from the sky.
The U.S. went to war because
The country wanted blood. I refused

To eat Campbell's Tomato Soup.
I hated George Bush and Karl Rove.

Now I'm 70 years old
And my grandson Johnny is watching
His hero Tom Brady go against
Peyton Manning and he's eating
Campbell's Tomato Soup.
"What're you thinking about, Poppa?"

"I'm thinking about Campbell's Tomato Soup.
It's finally just soup again.
That's all it is. Soup. Albeit bad soup.
Give me some.
I'll eat it if you sit and talk with me."
It's taken me all this time.

# THE END OF TOILET PAPER

This morning the toilet paper came to its conclusion.

The cardboard cylinder.

So I'm 5 years old.

I sit in the kitchen and toot my horn.

Toot toot.

Tula fixes me a peanut butter sandwich.

She laughs at me.

When she was a kid she had picked cotton.

She was good, she says, made money for her momma.

Not much, mind you, honey, nickels and dimes, but back then

Every little bit helped a whole lot.

But Tula hated the work.

It was dirty and hot.

They didn't have toilet paper.

Toot toot. Toot toot.

Tula had to go off in the trees and use the dirty leaves.

Little black girl going #2 in the bushes.

The white man knew where she was.

The white man knew where her mother was.

Tula never talked about her father.

Tula's grandparents had been slaves.

Her grandmother told Tula stories about Africa.

Where did those stories come from, Tula?

Be quiet, honey.

Africa was back there not so long ago.

                    Mother Africa.

# A SHORT DOCUMENTARY ABOUT A DEAD POET

*for Paul Malanga*

On a beautiful July day in 1955
Weldon Kees—
who was born in Beatrice, Nebraska, in 1914
and who received a modicum of fame
for his first book of poems
*The Last Man*
as well as his paintings which hung
briefly
at the Whitney
alongside work by Pablo Picasso—
parked his blue Plymouth Savoy
on the north side of the Golden Gate Bridge.
He left the keys in the ignition
and disappeared forever.
In his apartment, his friends found
his cat "Lonesome"
along with a pair of red socks in the sink.
His sleeping bag was gone.
So was his savings account book.

# A VARIATION ON A THEME BY JAMES SCHUYLER

*in memory of the painter Susan Klahr*


Standing and watching January out the back window
A grey comforter of winter clouds rests
On the Franklin Mountains and leaves
A white shadow of snow like a reminder
Of what I do not know the desert is so big

For looking into the east the blue sky opening up
A porn movie at the drive-in Mexico is at our backs be
Careful standing and watching the sparrows
And the finches argue about the seed in the feeder two
Juncos are happy enough finding their food

On the cold ground I wish some brown towhees
To the party I am always wanting more the yard
Is still so much undone buds on skeleton trees let
Us call them calacas I'm on the best of terms
With death she wanted to say but now it's too late.

# 1955

Frank Bevins was an old man in a raggedy brown suit.

A blue bow tie some days.

A red bow tie the next.

He rented the front room of Bennie's house.

She dyed her scraggly hair silver.

Her hand was paralyzed and useless.

It looked like a dead shrimp.

And her house smelled like old people.

Frank would take me to see the Memphis Chicks play ball.

Double-A Southern League.

1950s.

Birmingham Barons.

Atlanta Crackers.

Russwood Park on Union Avenue before it burned down.

Greasy popcorn and a Coca-Cola.

Frank would drink a beer.

Falstaff.

Frank liked to take a piss after the 4th inning.

"The 4th inning is the perfect time to piss," Frank said.

Russwood had those long white porcelain urinals,

All the men bellying up to piss elbow to elbow.

Frank unbuttoned his pants.

"Go ahead and take a pee, Bobby. A man needs to take a pee."

Frank pulled his penis out.

White baggy boxer shorts.

The thing was short and brown and shriveled.

He held it with the thumb and forefingers of his two hands.

He stared at the wall and enjoyed this pleasure.

It took a while.

He shook it when he was done and stuffed it back in.

Eisenhower was President.

I liked Ike. My father was dead.

Jackie Robinson was playing for the Dodgers.

The Dodgers were my team.

The men didn't talk about Jackie Robinson around me.

Frank made sure of that.

The lights were on, the grass was green—

Russwood Park was beautiful.

The great Luis Aparicio was shortstop.

A big guy named Ed White

Played center field for the Chicks forever.

Frank said poor old Ed would die in Memphis.

He couldn't hit a big league curve.

The black people had to sit on the other side

Of a fence down the 3rd base line.

It was crowded over there but they were having more fun.

# SUNDAY MORNING

Two old guys walk single file
Slowly and wordlessly around a room.
A white curtain filters the sunshine.
Outside is the hot desert sun.

The two men are shoeless. The smaller,
the guy in front, is limping because
40 years ago in Vietnam a kid in black pajamas
shot him in the head and almost killed him.

The other guy dodged that war,
lived in the mountains, lived in the city,
wife and three kids, drank a lot,
wrote some poems. A candle flickers,

incense burns. The floor is clean
because these two men cleaned it.
Three others were here but they left.
The man in front slaps two wooden

clappers together. The sound startles
the man behind. He takes a deep breath.
The men stop walking. The first man
Lights a stick of incense and places it

in front of a statue of the Buddha.
They bow to their cushions on the floor.
They sit down cross-legged and stare
at the wall. Their legs ache. It's been

three days now. Not much longer.
One of them is the teacher,
one of them the student. It doesn't
make much difference which is which.

# LUIS, GOD AND THE ONE-EYED CROW

*in memory of Luis Jimenez, 1941-2006*

The crow was sitting on top of a dead cottonwood tree,
Looking at God
And God turned around and snatched his eye.

God tossed the crow's eye into the Rio Ruidoso,
The noisy river, a mountain river
Traveling along until it disappeared into desert sand.

Let it be said that the eye that God snatched never got far,
But rotted
In the mud somewhere between Hondo and Roswell.

The crow flew up the canyon and sat down in another tree,
Suffered but
Eventually healed, leaving him to live beside the river

As a one-eyed crow who never looked in the face
Of God again.
He just kept doing his business which was being a crow.

"Life is like that sometimes," the crow said. Then one day
Luis came
Riding his appaloosa pony in that canyon. He found the crow

Dead inside a clump of long-stemmed grass. Luis
Shed a tear
For the one-eyed crow. Like the crow, Luis only had one eye.

When he was a boy, God had snatched Luis' eye in the alley
Behind his home.
Luis never forgot God's trick. He fashioned himself a hat

from the head of the crow. He put the crow hat on his head.
"That's what I do,"
He said. "I make things." Luis was a workingman artist

Doing his business. Like me, Luis was always angry
With God. God
In our stories was the same: the Father Who Went Away.

Maybe "God" is not the right word. Maybe "Father" is not
The right word. Luis
Was an artist, I am a poet. We have to use these tools

Given to us. Luis liked to ride his pony thru the scrub cedar,
Liked being alone
To admire the way the sun sets inside his one eye.

Luis carried his gun because he wanted to shoot God dead
If God gave him
The slightest chance, but God never showed his face again.

# MCDONALD'S™
*in memory of Artemisa Salinas (1932-2011)*

*The Great Way is not difficult for those who have no preferences.*
—Seng-T'san, the 3rd Patriarch

I got a Zen friend eats vegetarian at MacDonald's sometimes. He likes the cheap coffee. He says, "Don't be a snob, Bobby. What difference does it make?" And he gives me a wise Buddhist smile.

I tell my friend if I'm going to eat fast food, then I'm going to eat at some local place. Like the H&H Carwash over on Yandell. The Haddads own the place, Kenny and Maynard. 4th generation Lebanese Christian immigrants. Both right wingers, but they leave me alone.

I tell my friend that the 3rd Patriarch eats there too. He likes the spinning stools at the counter. He's a vegetarian too so he orders the chili relleno plate. It's way too much food of course. He wants just enough, so he takes his leftovers to the bum in the alley.

The bum's name is Chuy, short for Jesus. Kenny doesn't like the 3rd Patriarch feeding Chuy. "It's like attracting flies," Kenny says. Seng-T'san smiles at Kenny's rant but he will do as he pleases. Chuy needs to eat. "Yeah, yeah," Kenny says and walks away.

The rellenos are delicious as always. Likewise the refried beans and fried potatoes. A couple of tortillas de maiz. On the side a glass of water and a cup of coffee.

Seng-T'san is no dummy. Gloria the cook fries the rellenos and everything else in a little bit of lard. Oh well. He eats what's set before him. Gloria is a tiny woman, and she comes from across the border to cook our rellenos. Seng-T'san smiles at Gloria, his hands in gassho.

Then he gives thanks to all the other many beings who have brought this food to his table. Even the pig who provided the lard. In his thanksgiving he saves Artemisa the waitress for last. She's his favorite and he understands deeply he's not supposed to have favorites. But Artemisa has such a beautiful big smile.

She says "De nada" and "Quieres más?" She always pours extra coffee to keep his cup warm and makes sure everything is perfect. Then she leaves him alone while he eats. She likes gringos okay and a Chinaman is just another kind of gringo. This one eats everything and always leaves a big tip.

The coffee is lousy but that's okay.

# IMPERIALISM IN THE 21ST CENTURY: THE BUSH YEARS

George Bush flew to Pakistan.

They hated George Bush in Pakistan.

With good reason.

George carries his bible like an AK-47.

The Muslims carry the Koran the same way.

It was them against us, us against them.

But Mohammed

He paid George no never-mind.

The prophet fed the president bitter pomegranates.

The president refused.

He didn't want his lips purple with the juices.

Lee changed the channel.

Kathryn Hepburn was pulling leeches off poor Humphrey Bogart.

The African Queen was lost in the swamps and the reeds.

Life always happens like this. There is no story without trouble.

Kathryn Hepburn was undaunted.

Humphrey Bogart was in love.

The Germans, like the American Empire, didn't stand a chance.

# THE LESSONS OF MY MOTHER

In the walled city of Monte Vista in the Italian hills east of Lucca, Giuseppe's beautiful high-heeled wife bends to serve me the chateaubriand for two. She's happy to show me her healthy tan breasts. This is part of her service.

•

My mother on her knees bent over her bed, her hands cupped together, praying. Sometimes to God, sometimes to Billy—dead husband, dead father. What happened to her sex life? I'm on I-10 to Los Angeles. Mecca, the sign says, is 20 miles that way. Comanche Springs is 15 miles the other way.

•

I have a friend, a socialist, who lives half his life on a little island in the blue Caribbean Sea. He says it's paradise. The people are poor and they know they are poor but that's okay. They are happy. They have all that they need. My friend the socialist said that he has lost the art of metaphor. He's studying the art of happiness. That is exactly what he said. But what happens when he comes home for the other half of his life?

•

A mouse ran across Lee's bare feet in the kitchen and she screamed. I baited a trap with peanut butter. Sitting in the living room reading a poem I heard the trap snap shut, the mouse squeal and die. A tiny drop of blood on the linoleum.

•

My memories are like a man who's forbidden to return to Czechoslovakia or who's afraid to return to Argentina. Right now has to be good enough. It's all that I have. An antlered deer was standing atop my car. Two barn owls—winged night beasts ghostly white—flopped on the ground, belly up and soon to be dead.

•

Jill always wanted to be a painter like Pollock or Rothko but she was afraid to be a painter. Then she had a baby, her thighs trembling, the terrible pain, her mind sure she would die, sure the baby would die, but her body of its own accord did everything needed to be done—a labor and art form at which she excelled. She had left her thinking behind. Forgot the yes and no. She just did what was necessary. No decisions to make. And so she became a painter.

# THE LESSONS OF MY FATHER

The urethra is the canal through which urine is discharged from the bladder in most mammals and through which semen is discharged in the male. For the male the urethra passes through the prostate like the tunnel on the mountain road to Cloudcroft.

•

It was morning, November 26th, 1919. Pancho Villa was camped in the desert and Felipe Angeles sat on a bed in a jail cell. He was going to die soon. The men in the firing squad were cleaning their rifles. Felipe had made his speech, he had forgiven the executioners, he had written his wife Carlita, he was dressed in the black suit the Revilla family had given him and he was ready to die.

•

Welcome to the bowels of desire. A river flowed by the house. The house had a wide screened-in front porch and a huge oak tree shaded it from the sun. My dreams have been in search of my soul but they have come up empty. They take refuge in the body. My father loved airplanes and wanted to own a Piper Cub dealership after the war. No such luck. What would have happened if he had lived? But that not really a question to answer. My father was dead for all these many years. I have forgiven him. I harvested the last of the basil and made pesto for dinner. The pesto needed more garlic—that's what my daughter said.

•

Once I didn't think of myself as a riddle with a mouth and a nose and other appliances. She—that forever "she," my muse, all the women in my life, my father's muse—means, here we are. Are we waiting for another war? Whatever is going to happen is already happening. What is there to break down? A panic attack is a door opening. No, that's not right. It's a Chinese traffic light.

•

The man in the black suit had already disappeared. Like he was in the wrong movie. The plot was all wrong. She got a Coca-Cola with lime. The Sunni man said the Shia men killed his friends at the checkpoint because of George Bush. Sex was impossible. Everything turned into writing. Well, not everything. When the gunslinger was in the town of Kal, his girlfriend told him she had asked the man in the black suit what death was like. He told her point blank "the number 19." There's no such number in a cribbage game. The gunslinger shot her in the forehead.

•

They were not man and wife. Anybody could tell that. A man and a wife wear each other like underwear. She was a prostitute. Three of us went to a flea market. The business cards fell chaotically onto the floor. Her husband was taking the kids out. They lived upstairs, locked up most of the time. I decided to eat a steak, even though I am a vegetarian. The flowers are fake; the music is lousy. This is what money does.

•

The one lousy bloom on the Christmas cactus is red and
glorious. It's January already.

•

A car stunned a robin on Richmond. I stopped and picked up the
shuttering bird in my hands and planted her again in a juniper
tree. A drop of blood in my urine. A pressure on my asshole. The
doctor looks at me and thinks.

•

The Plaza Theatre. 1955. Memphis, Tennessee. William Holden
rode the rails into a quiet Kansas community hoping his wealthy
college chum would offer him a "respectable" job. Kim Novak
came down the staircase. I fell in love. Andre Previn wrote the
music. Benign enlargement of the prostate. White clouds float
through the windows.

•

The nurse comes in and tells me to take off my pants. She cleans
my penis and wipes it with a disinfecting jell. She inserts a tube
deep into the urethra. She covers me with a white sheet and tells
me the doctor will be in soon. She refuses to look at me. Tick.
Tock. The doctor comes in with a big smile. It's his turn now. He
inserts a tiny filament into the tube. The tip of the filament is a
camera. He says, "You will feel cold water, you will feel

pressure." I can see inside my bladder. The bladder is a beautiful place to be. The doctor says the bladder is a muscle. "Nothing is wrong, but it could be better."

# WHERE IS THAT BEETLE GOING?

Some kind of dung beetle,
One of those flat black beetles
The size of my fingernail
Walked across the red gravel,
Down the concrete curb
And under the car,
Disappearing into the nowhere,
Wherever that is.
"Bobby," my wife yelled
At me from the porch,
"Dinner is ready,
Don't sit out there forever."

# I MAKE A GOOD POT OF BEANS

Christians like my beans.
Right-wing, left-wing—they like my beans.
Buddhists like my beans.
Muslims and Jews like my beans.
Agnostics and atheists.
Mexicans and gringos.
Vegetarians and meat eaters.
Phyllis and Bill like my beans.
Does Megan like my beans?
Yes, yes, Megan likes my beans.
They all like my beans.
Even the drunks down the street like my beans.
And I know some politicians who like my beans.
Likewise some ex-cons and thieves.
Friends of mine.
All of them.
Poets of course like my beans.
Perhaps some novelists.
Who knows?
A few holy men, a few holy women
(Not too many wise folks out there—
Be careful who you listen to.)
My kids and grandkids like my beans.
My wife likes my beans.
She really likes it when I cook my beans.
Write me a letter.

A real letter the old fashioned way—
Buy a stamp. A postcard.
I'll send you the recipe for my beans.

# PLEASE . . .

*in memory of Wayne Crawford*

Let me say that Wayne has gone away
Let me read his dead poet poems
Let me fry these other fish
Please let me stuff myself with fagioli
Let me parsley and parmesan
Let me and all poets tell their story
Let Wayne tell his story
How it began in one place and it ends in another
Please take a tip from me
Please let me put the pieces back together
Please let me Howdy Doody
Let me Buffalo Bob and Clarabelle too
Let me Muddy Waters and Jimmy Reed
Let me Li Po and Wang Wei
And, like Wayne, let me Superman and let me Lois too
Please let me look inside that closet door
Let me say goodbye please let me say hello
Yes hello
Goodbye too
Please let the light shine inside
The sunlight and the candlelight
The light to read a book by
Just a little bit of light for lovemaking
Light for the flute light for the song

Light to sing along

Light

More light

Less light and so

No light

Wayne has left the light the room the house

He has gone outside

He has emptied his pockets

He has said goodbye

The light is gone from his eyes

Please let us say goodbye

And yes

Oh when the time does come

Please let us all go through that door with grace

Please let us be excused

Please let us go outside

Let the light be exhausted from our eyes

Please

Please let us go you and me

Let us be excused let us go outside

And thank you yes thank you

Thank you thank you

Thank you Wayne thank you

You have gone outside

Thank you

And so goodbye

# A SONNET FOR LOVE

Flossie put her plums in the icebox.
Bill ate a plum and wrote a famous poem.
I tried the same trick on my wife.
Turns out she doesn't like cold fruit.
That's what she said.
She turned over and went to sleep.
That was afterwards.
I got up twice in the night to pee.
At 5am she let the cat in and fed him.
When she climbed back into bed she farted.
We giggled and went back to sleep.
After a while she let the cat back out and made coffee.
Sometimes I do all that stuff but it's so nice when she does it.
This poem, like all of my poems, is for sale.

## MESSAGE TO GRANDKIDS

Toilets are eloquent.
And they speak the truth.
Remember that.

# FOUR NEW YORK CITY POEMS
## MAY 2011

*1. What Was Supposed to Happen Didn't Happen*

The world was supposed to end yesterday
But Paul and Timothy got it wrong
They talked to God to see where their math went askew
God said the End of the World needs more juice
Juice like that jazz sextet at the African Market on 116*th*
The other side of Malcolm X
Three black guys on the brass horns talking Age of Aquarius
Zulu
Piano Cuban talks back voodoo bebop mojo
Middle-aged Jewish drummer guy in a wife-beater
Translates the Word
Skinny Asian American woman thumping the standup bass

My gosh, *how did she get here?*

Maybe this is the End of the World
No wonder the Muslims are praising Allah on their prayer rugs
Ignoring that ancient Japanese guy slurping at his noodles
Rumor is that the old man is enlightened
Although you'd never guess it
He's eyeing the young women of poetry
Lesbians or straight he has no preferences
They are wearing skirts, they're wearing naked legs

Their hips sway to keep time with the music
They prophesy the Ying and the Yang

—Thank you, Ladies! Thank you!

The rhythms and the riffs are our gate into the meadow
Summertime and the living is easy, sweetheart,
Yes maybe the world has already ended
Maybe we're the last to know

*2. The Number 104 Headed North on Broadway*

Strange how Ron Padgett is getting so long-winded
I'm glad
Lorenzo Thomas is glad too
In fact, I wish Lorenzo was writing this poem
But dead people can't write poems
Not even in New York City
That's a good reason to be sad
On a beautiful spring day with so many poppies
The poppies are delicious
I know the poppies are delicious because
A hummingbird just flitted by
She disappeared into the leafy branches of a sweet gum
Here comes a blue helmeted cop atop his horse
Clop clop clop clop
A 3-legged dog is attached to a bow-legged woman
The dog is white the woman is black
This is the Map of the World, Lee said
We cannot come close to imagining the suffering of others
Then the French tourists left the bus

4 men
3 women
3 toddlers
2 babies

What a bus ride!

Hello, Ron
Goodbye, Lorenzo
It's been just too too

*3. Before you turn out the light, spread some mayonnaise*
*on my bread*

The three bean chili at the Hale & Hearty
On Lexington @ 64*th*
Is okay but they don't give you a pot to piss in
Me I could wait this time so I looked out the window
Those people over there are waiting for the bus
Why should I be apprehensive?
Among them is a man named Sam
Like Art in America
I don't know Art from Adam
That was a long time ago
Him and Eve
At least in New York City
Please pay attention to the words
And say goodbye to Sam, Adam and Art
They all got on the bus together
Matisse has this luscious nude floating by
She's laying her bare bottom on cold blue tiles
Maybe lie down beside her
Keep her warm and dry
Henri had faith in the Garden
I have faith in the Garden
This is the real meaning of America
What is that, a yellow balloon?

## 4. Bus Ride

#66 goes through and to the other side
East Side and West Side
On both sides is 66th
In the middle is the beautiful park
Let's say the park is emptiness
Because it's night so dark and full
The trees the grasses the birds the bugs
The realm of luminous beings who live above and beneath
Feral cats
A wilderness
An ontology of wilderness
But not perfect
"Perfect" is such a lousy word
Let's call it
Improvisational ecology
Where everything is okay
Because
Who knows what's going to happen?
Words don't work anyway
Except as decoration and companionship

Tonight I'm glad

For confusion and contradiction
Especially now
I am old enough to know

There's never any reason to hurt anybody

No reason to kill anybody

Although it keeps happening all around

Like a disease

Please

I whisper to the muse of my poems

(She's in the bus somewhere

I know she is)

I whisper, let's go home now

I'll go to my house you go to your house

Say hello to your lover for me

I hope you have a lover

If you don't, be at peace love yourself

I'll see you tomorrow if I can find you

I've learned during all these years

That the bus must turn around and go the other way

# HOUSEFLIES

I read in some lost Zen Buddhist book that the mind
is like a housefly, the way it flits around here and there.
I remembered that little tidbit this morning when
I found a housefly that got stuck all night in the fridge.
The housefly was sitting atop the milk carton.
It was still alive.
Poor tiny beast.
And it was an easy kill—
I grabbed it between my thumb and forefinger.
It was cold to the touch and I felt its thorax crack.

## DEAR HARVEY,

We never did straighten out our friendship,
But it was you, back when we were 16 years old,
Who first opened all these doors for me—
Poems. The magic of language.
The power of stories and myths.
So here I am in Seattle, on a business trip,
But I'm really looking for your ghost.
I want to say goodbye.
I got these nice hotel digs on 6th & Seneca
Up the hill from the Pike Street Market.
In the bathroom I found a long turd and his little brother
Residing in the toilet bowl like
The punctuation of bad omens.
The television said Patty Hearst
Is raising a French bulldog named Diva.
I went out walking in the cold Seattle rain.
One old bum, sure he could have been you,
Tall and skinny, wrapped in a beat-up poncho,
Straggling off toward Belltown in the drizzle.
Why did you stay in this town? The winters seem
So full of sorrow. A bowl of clam chowder, some beer
I'm being an old man now, just like you,

Except you're dead. The screen on my laptop blinked.
My muse was staring at me. This time she was Jewish or maybe
Lebanese.

She looked like Stephanie. You never met Stephanie, did you?
My Jewish girlfriend that was so long ago.
The muse stared at me sideways, pressing her eyeball
against the computer screen. What did she see?

> *Benign Prostatic hyperplasia.*
> *Teeth missing.*
> *Medicated blood pressure.*
> *Varicose veins in both legs.*

All the useless secrets of this river, this ocean,
this emptiness? She sat back in her chair and took off
her cashmere sweater one button at a time.

She said,

> *The thing you call yourself is not real.*

Looking at me sideways in a black lacy bra.
She reached behind her back with that wonderful facility
of a woman's hands, and unhooked the snaps and the bra
fell away into the wherever it is, the ether, where
muses populate the universe.

I could no longer see her face.
I could not see the mystery of her hands,
only the large teardrops of her breasts, the ancient coin
of her nipples. Bits of her chin.
Her long neck writhing like a snake, she disappeared.

This is the 21st Century.
These mysteries flourish like your friends,
those homeless men searching for a place to dry off
and get warm in the alleys of Seattle. I miss you.
Please send me news.

Love,
Bobby

## LYING IN BED AFTER LOVEMAKING

We can't be any more naked than this.
No wonder this is called the Little Death.
Who were those two people anyway?

# SUMMERTIME WISHBONE

Did it myself.
Cracked it in two.
Got the big bone.
Got the little bone.
I wished to be
Enlightened big-time
But down-the-street
Robert Garza
Asked Lee to help with
His tapioca pudding.
Lee told him
She doesn't do
Tapioca pudding.
Eddie Natividad sat on the curb
With a quart of Bud-Lite
Between his legs like a lover.
Eddie gets drunk
When he's happy, gets
Drunk when he's sad.
The daylight finally went away
Behind the mountain,
And suddenly,
I'm just this old man
Pissing in the backyard
Darkness, a poor excuse
For an enlightened man.

Oh, I don't worry. Wishes,
Like days, are forever
Falling away. Better
To enjoy these rain clouds
Filling up the sky, the desert
Always needs the rain.
I can hear and feel the first
Few drops—so delicious!
Thank you, chicken.
Thank you, rain.

# VALENTINE'S DAY 2011

Lee had hip replacement surgery
at the hospital the same week
the people of Egypt twittered
Hosni Mubarak aside a people's

revolution on the computer screen
when 300 real people
died Herodotus said that Egypt
is the gift of the River Nile
Anwar Sadat crossed the Suez
Canal the prophet Moses slept
in a basket afloat in its reeds
that night I didn't dream
of the Pyramids
but a man was cutting through
the muscle of her leg sawed the bone
into two pieces little white worms filled
the bloody mess 3 am I woke up
in a cold sweat stumbled to the bathroom
Happy Valentine's Day, my love
we grow older together and you are so
wonderfully beautiful and this is how we practice
for the end of our days when the universe
will welcome us home

# THIS MORNING I MADE LOVE WITH THE LETTUCE PICKER

Every year the lettuce picker plants her seeds in October.
Lettuce loves October in the Chihuahua Desert.
October passes and November comes.
The lettuce grows leafy and happy.
The lettuce picker slips out to the garden in the morning.
I will not tell you how old I am.
I will not tell you how old she is.
But her legs are white, her rear end
is clad in purple pajamas
and is raised like a flag planted
in the dirt
for the preservation of love.
Today is Sunday, the day of Sabbath.
A day to remember ourselves.
A day to worship all that is holy.
This is what we do when we make love.

## MEMO, #34

"Getting old is like…
well,
it's like getting old."

That's what I told her.
She laughed.

I guess it follows that death
Will be like death.

But I didn't say that.

Our dinner was black beans and a salad.
Cornbread baked in a cast-iron skillet with lots of butter.
Real butter.
We split a bottle of red wine from somewhere in Spain.
Now I've washed all the dinner dishes.
That's my job.
She's asleep.
And the November moon is almost full.

## PLEASE WAIT

Thank you for calling.

All of our agents are currently assisting other customers.

Please remain on the line.

The next available customer representative will be with you

shortly.

# { ENDNOTES }

### KENSHŌ DOWN ON TEXAS AVENUE, EL PASO, TEXAS
Kenshō is a Japanese Zen Buddhist term that literally means "seeing one's nature" or "true self." Kenshō experiences are tiered, in that they escalate from initial glimpses into the nature of mind, on to a complete experience of the emptiness of the universe.

### LA LUZ DE LA RESISTENCIA—A LIGHT POEM IN MEMORY OF RAUL SALINAS
I wrote this poem during the week of 3.11.08 after Raul's death. I had been reading Jackson Mac Low's aleatoric contrived poems—"The Light Poems"—in his book *A Thing of Beauty*. I was moved deeply by his Dead Mother poems.

### THE LESSONS OF MY MOTHER
Thanks to the great Israeli poet Yehuda Amichai for his Czechoslovakia and Argentina poems. They are the inspiration for these oblique impressions and memories of my mother and father. The painter Jill Somoza enters the poem with a brush and a story about the birthing of babies and the making of art. That story remains, after all this time, vital to my understanding about how I make poems. Also, thanks to Lisa Gill, Stephen King, Joan Logge, David Romo and the ghosts of Dogen and Ted Berrigan. I randomly snatched pieces of their work from the journal I was using to compose this poem.

### FOUR NEW YORK CITY POEMS
Thanks to my good friends John and Sylvia Gardner who for several years in the month of May have given me a place to stay on the Upper West Side. For a little bit of time, I can be totally engaged as a poet. I walk the streets. I ride the subways and the busses. I carry a notebook around, jotting down images and bits of conversations. I read poetry books. I go to readings, museums and performances. When it's time to go home, I go home. I'm always happy to go home.

### BEFORE YOU TURN OUT THE LIGHT, SPREAD SOME MAYONNAISE ON MY BREAD
Number 3 of the "Four New York City Poems," the title is the title of one of artist James Magee's "Titles." I heard Jim perform his "Titles" at Hunter College (May 2011) with aleatoric composer Bob Ostertag. A beautiful performance. Beforehand I was hungry so I got the big bowl of 3 lentil soup at the Hale and Hearty. A bus came by advertising a Matisse Exhibition. I jotted down notes. I wrote most of this poem on the bus ride home. I love mayonnaise.

# { THE COVER PHOTO }

The cover photo—with its Edward Hopper "Night Hawks" ambiance—
is by César Ivan, and the plywood cutout installation in the window is
his too. The installation was at the Bridge Center for Contemporary
Art in downtown El Paso around 2001. The Bridge was a crucible for
El Paso's leading-edge arts scene in the 1990s into the early 2000s.
A true laboratory of the imagination for me and so many others. Many
thanks to its director David Romo and Board Chair Fred Dalbin for
keeping the beast alive as long as they did.

FROM RIGHT TO LEFT—

*Gloria Osuna Perez (1947-1999)*—Chicana artist and ceramicist.
Also, a life-long activist in support of Chicano and human rights.
Gloria was a courageous woman in her art, politics and life. And, most
remarkably, in facing her death. Lee and I knew her the last few years
of her life as she battled ovarian cancer. Thinking her cancer was in
remission, she agreed to work with Cinco Puntos to illustrate Joe

Hayes' book, *Little Gold Star / La estrellita del oro*. She completed the sketches and three of the paintings when the cancer returned with a vengeance. From her deathbed, she passed along her very special techniques and the project to her daughter Lucia Angela Perez.

*Teresa Urrea, la Teresita, la Santa de Cabora (1873-1906)*—Historian and arts activist David Romo first introduced me to the history of la Teresita when he was doing research for his book *Ringside Seat to a Revolution*. She was a healer, mystic, and, according to the Diaz Regime, an insurgent leader against the Mexican government. She lived in El Paso in the late 1880s after being banished from Mexico. Read Luis Alberto Urrea's excellent novel *The Hummingbird's Daughter* for a fictionalized history of the early part of her life.

*Art Lewis (1937-2012)*—The late, great and legendary saxophonist continues to blow his horn in the ambiente of downtown El Paso. He was my friend and a wise man. When we first moved here, Lee and I heard Art playing his bluesy jazz at Kiki's on Piedras Street. I felt like I was home. You can always find Art Lewis in my poems.

*Pancho Villa (1878-1923)*—He frequently crossed into El Paso during the early 1900s and even lived here for a while. Villa, like Teresita, is one of the ghosts that wander through the dreams and mythos of El Paso and the border.

That's me on the left. I am honored to be included. I'm still alive. For the time being.

# { ACKNOWLEDGMENTS }

I'm a lucky guy. I have a bunch of friends who support and inspire me in all the odds and ends of my daily life. I want to thank them all, but, in particular, those friends who had an impact on the making of this book.

- Connie Voisine, friend and Poem Doctor Supreme.

- Joe Somoza and JB Bryan. Poem buddies, life buddies. JB designed this book.

- Joe Hayes. Close friend and confidante.

- Johnny Byrd. Son, good friend and CFO/Co-Editor at Cinco Puntos. He always advises Lee and me to take a deep breath.

- My Zen buddies—my teacher Harvey Daiho Hilbert Roshi (founder of the Order of Clear Mind Zen), my colleagues Polly Shikan Perez and Kathryn Shukke Masaryk, and all the members of our sangha at Both Sides / No Sides Zen Community here in El Paso.

*Bobby Byrd (1942)* grew up in Memphis, Tennessee, during the Golden Age of that city's music scene. "Black music, or *race music* as it was called, the great DJ Dewey Phillips and WDIA radio," he says, "probably saved my life." He and his wife Lee got together in 1967. After much meandering and close to twenty different addresses, they and their three kids moved to El Paso in 1978. They felt at home. The author of numerous books of poetry, Byrd has received a National Endowment of Arts Fellowship, the D.H. Lawrence Fellowship awarded by the University of New Mexico, an International Residency Fellowship awarded jointly by the National Endowment for the Arts and el Instituto de Belles Artes de México, and the Southwest Book Award. In 1985, Lee and Bobby founded Cinco Puntos Press in the Five Points Neighborhood of El Paso. In 2005, they each received a Cultural Freedom Fellowship from the Lannan Foundation for their work as publishers in supporting intellectual diversity and multi-cultural literature. In 2010, Byrd was ordained as a Zen Priest in the Order of Clear Mind Zen. He does make a good pot of beans.

## MORE GOOD COOKING FROM CINCO PUNTOS PRESS

*Beauty is a Verb: The New Poetry of Disability*
edited by Jennifer Bartlett, Sheila Black and Michael Northen

*Incantations: Songs, Spells and Images by Mayan Women*
edited by Ambar Past, Xalik Guzmán Bakbolom
and Xperta Ernandes

*The Resurrection of Bert Ringold*
Harvey Goldner

*White Panties, Dead Friends & Other Bits & Pieces of Love*
Bobby Byrd

*The Price of Doing Business in Mexico*
Bobby Byrd

*On the Transmigration of Souls in El Paso*
Bobby Byrd

**CINCO PUNTOS PRESS**
701 Texas Avenue   El Paso, TX  79901
915-838-1625
www.cincopuntos.com